PEDEZ THE PENGUIN AND THE MAGIC ICE TRAY

A Parable By Wealthykids.org

Written by Tony A. Gaines and Shaana D Ramos
Illustration by Tony A. Gaines and Shaana D. Ramos
ALL Rights reserved @ Copyright Tony A Gaines and
Shaana D. Ramos for Wealthykids.org
Disclaimer

Published by Wealthykids.org
8175 Limonite Avenue Suite A
Riverside, CA 92509
sarahwealthinc@gmail.com

GRAINS FOR GROWTH!

One Day While Walking down Knowledge Iceberg Shore,

Pedez Found A Magic Ice Cube Tray.

He picked up two ice cubes and when he looked inside,

The Magic ice cubes let him see into the future.

Then Pedez made glasses from the ice cubes,

And shared them with his friends.

Now ALL of His friends can now see the future!

Pedez began to build a company,

He Named the Company Penguin Financial.

Pedez and his friends turn their place into Penguin's Island,

And now deliver many products all over the globe.

The Meaning
Of The Parable
- One To
Grow On!

A Parable by Wealthykids.org

A Dream is The key to a great idea .

Ideas are a gift from God.

Once The Idea has been activated,

It will unleash opportunity forever.

The idea will help you to expand Opportunity and give products to share

To benefit both family and friends.

Now All of your family and friends will start dreaming

And create ideas for themselves

To share with others all over the world!

FINI

PEDEZ THE PENGUIN
AND THE MAGIC
ICE TRAY
A Parable By Wealthykids.org

Written by Shaana D Ramos and Tony A. Gaines
Illustration by Shaana D. Ramos and Tony A. Gaines
ALL Rights reserved @ Copyright Shaana D. Ramos and Tony A. Gaines
for Wealthykids.org

Published by Wealthykids.org
8175 Limonite Avenue suite A
Riverside, CA 92509
sarahwealthinc@gmail.com

www.ingramcontent.com/pod-product-compliance
Lightning Source LLC
Chambersburg PA
CBHW041622180526
45159CB00002BC/969